THE DOG TRAINING PACK

Learn to Train Your Dog in Just 10 Minutes a Day!

Sarah Whitehead

RONNIE
SELLERS
PRODUCTIONS
PORTLAND, MAINE

First edition published in North America by

Ronnie Sellers Productions, Inc.

P.O. Box 818, Portland, Maine 04104

For ordering information:

(800) 625-3386 toll-free

(207) 772-6814 fax

Visit our Web sites: www.rsvp.com or

www.makefun.com

E-mail: rsp@rsvp.com

Ronnie Sellers President and Publisher

Robin Haywood Publishing Director

Mary Baldwin Production Editor

Jessica Curran Associate Editor

This book was conceived, designed, and produced by

THE IVY PRESS LIMITED

The Old Candlemakers

Lewes, East Sussex BN7 2NZ, UK

Creative Director Peter Bridgewater

Publisher Sophie Collins

Editorial Director Jason Hook

Art Director Karl Shanahan

Senior Project Editor Caroline Earle

Design The Lanaways

Illustrator Tony Walter-Bellue

ISBN: 1-56906-589-6

10 9 8 7 6 5 4 3 2 1

Printed and bound in China

Contents

Introduction

The dog has been our companion for thousands of years. He has acted as hunting partner, working colleague in the field, as our eyes and ears, and as protector in the home. Above all, the dog is an excellent member of the family, fitting in with our daily routines and sharing our lives in a way that no other pet can.

Dogs are our friends, and the basis of that friendship is good communication.

However, dogs will be dogs! They bark, they dig, they jump up, and chew! It is up to us to show them how to behave in our homes and as part of the wider community. Effective, positive training will allow your dog freedom and expression. It's a pleasure to be able to take your dog with you if he's well-behaved; and of course, his behavior will reflect on the time and effort you have put into his education.

The Dog Training Pack is guaranteed to make a difference in just 10 minutes a day, whether you're faced with a cute but misbehaving puppy or a recalcitrant adult dog. To give responsible, but time-poor dog owners everything they need, the pack contains the following items to help turn your dog into a cooperative player.

Our best friend

Whether you hope to train your dog as a worker, or simply as a loving companion, understanding his behavior will enrich your relationship and make your learning journey together fun and lasting.

Clicker

The ultimate training tool. Clicker training is one of the most modern methods, chosen by professional dog trainers for its ease of use, speed in training, and kindness. In only a few minutes your dog will be able to understand that the click means he's done the right thing and that a reward is coming.

Whistle

Traditionally used as a signal to call your dog back to you, it is invaluable in the home and field. Easily transferable between family members and consistent for your dog.

Tug toy

All dogs love to play, and this tug toy can be used as a reward to enhance training and to build your relationship with your dog. The fun squeaker will keep your dog amused for hours!

Training book

In just 10 minutes a day, you can train your dog to become a valued and well-behaved member of the family. Use this book to get your relationship off to a great start and to launch your dog's training program. This book contains lots of ideas for all the family to follow, including basic training, tricks for fun, and more advanced tasks for dog geniuses!

Understanding Your Dog

Dogs don't speak English! Dogs see, hear, feel, and smell the world around them quite differently from us. Because of this we have to teach them the meaning of every word that we want them to understand. Learning to understand your dog's body language will reduce the likelihood of misunderstanding each other.

Dogs communicate using body language and facial expressions. They also make a range of sounds, and have the advantage of being able to "read" each other — and us — via their heightened sense of smell.

Learning the lingo

Bear in mind that dogs don't experience guilt! Instead, a dog will typically respond to being scolded by putting his ears back, his tail down, and holding his body low to the ground. These are all signs of fear.

Bounces

Some puppies bounce, so that their two front feet pounce simultaneously toward another puppy. Puppies will sometimes bounce, then run away, which is an invitation to chase them.

Hip swing

Some dogs, particularly larger breeds, like to sidle up to other dogs and then spin around quickly, knocking the other dog gently with its hips. By turning its back, the dog shows that it means no harm and is inviting play.

Play bow

Here the dog puts his head low to the ground and his bottom and tail high in the air, as if he is going to pounce. This shows an intention to play and is often copied by other dogs.

Paw raises

The dog raises his paw in a floppy-elbowed fashion, pawing at the air, or sometimes patting another dog. This is a clear play signal — the dog means no harm.

Hackles up

Puppies often have raised hackles (the hair on the back of the neck) when they are experiencing insecurity and excitement. In an adult dog, raised hackles may be a warning of impending aggression.

Confidence and nervousness

When your dog is confident, it is likely that his ears will be up and alert, his tail will be up, and his movement will be fluid and positive. If he is nervous, the chances are his ears will be pinned right back, and he will make himself look as small as possible by shrinking toward the ground and tucking his tail underneath him.

Eyes

Direct and head-on staring is nearly always interpreted as a threat. Dogs need to learn early on that averting their gaze when greeting a new dog is a safe behavior that will keep them out of trouble. Their mother will have started to teach them this in the litter, by staring hard at them if they behave inappropriately and following up this stare with a snap or growl if necessary.

Ears

Ear positions are important for canine communication. Unfortunately, the messages are often confused with dogs selectively bred to have long, pendulous ears. However, in breeds that have highly mobile, upright ears, the messages are easy to read. Ears pointed upright and forward show that the dog is alert and ready for action. Ears held back, or pinned to the head, show that the dog is in a high state of anxiety or fear.

How dogs learn

Dogs are like people: they need motivation and rewards in order to learn and do what you ask. Teaching your dog using kindness, praise, and rewards will mean he will enjoy learning, making the whole process faster and simpler. Remember, what gets rewarded, gets repeated!

Why use food and toys?

Some owners believe that a dog should do what they tell it because it "loves" them. This is like saying that we should go to work every day for the love of the company — or our boss! Dogs certainly need to learn that praise is rewarding but, while this can be a powerful tool, the vast majority of dogs need more of a "salary" to motivate them. Find out what your dog prefers — small pieces of tasty food or a favorite toy are usually best.

Clicker training

Clicker training is one of the most effective training methods available — and it is fun for both you and your dog. You do not have to push, pull, or force your dog to do anything. In this method of training, you only ever touch your dog with your hands in a positive way, to indicate praise.

What is a clicker?

A clicker is a small plastic box that contains a tiny sheet of flexible steel. When pressed, this sheet makes a distinctive "click-click" sound. Over a very short period of time, your dog can learn to associate this sound with getting food, toys, and praise — in other words, rewards for good behavior. This sound then "marks" the behavior that got the reward, much like putting a gold star on a page next to schoolwork well done!

Timing skills

Using the clicker makes the timing of rewards much easier for both dog and handler to understand. It clearly indicates to the dog why he got the reward and means that he can be creative and use his brain to discover what achieves the sound, and what doesn't.

Dogs that become "clicker-wise" can perform amazing training feats. In fact, many of the assistance-dog organizations that train dogs to help their disabled owners — by turning lights on and off, operating elevator buttons, and bringing in the milk, for example — train using clicker principles.

Your dog is bound to make mistakes at first. These do not represent failure — only feedback. If you ask your dog to sit, and he refuses, he is not being naughty, but is lacking in motivation or simply does not understand what you are saying. Ignore his mistakes — just don't click or treat — and he will soon figure out that only the responses you are looking for will bring him rewards.

One of the joys of clicker training is that it's so quick to bring results. In just 10 minutes a day, you too can have a dog to be proud of!

Starting Off: A New Puppy

Getting a new puppy is exciting, and will inevitably mean a change to your family's routine. Make sure, however, that you don't become a slave to the newcomer. Establish some sensible guidelines in your household from the outset — and then stick to them!

Dogs love predictable routines. Sticking to the same times for feeding and exercise will help your puppy become housebroken more quickly and make him feel more secure. Include quiet times during the daily routine so that your puppy learns when it is appropriate to demand attention. Establishing a basic pattern will help him to settle into his new home and make him less likely to be disruptive.

Handle with care

Handle and groom your puppy all over for at least 10 minutes every day. This can be one of the most effective ways to teach a puppy to be calm around people and to enjoy human touch. Dogs that are deprived of physical contact with people early on can take longer to form bonds when they become adults, and can be more difficult to train and examine. Handling should always be gentle and pleasant for your puppy, so use firm but quite gentle strokes. Just like us, dogs love a massage!

Meeting and greeting

● Teach your puppy how to greet people politely by encouraging him to sit when saying hello to visitors and people outside. Ignore rowdy behavior by keeping him on the leash when visitors first arrive, and praise and reward calm greetings. Avoid situations where your puppy is likely to get overexcited and difficult to control. For example, you could use a baby gate to contain your puppy if children will be running around!

● Try not to interfere when your dog says hello to another. Keep the leash loose and give the dogs space to sniff each other and interact naturally.

House rules

Your dog's dictionary

Choose the words that you want your puppy to respond to. Dogs don't understand the meaning of words themselves. Instead, they need to be taught to associate particular commands with actions, and this means being consistent. Write a list of the words you are going to use with your puppy, and what each one means, and then stick it to the refrigerator door. That way the whole family will use the same commands and you won't confuse your puppy.

A good start

It's all too easy to allow your puppy to get away with murder when he's small and cute — but don't allow him to establish behaviors that you'll regret later on. Letting your puppy sleep on the couch may seem acceptable when he's eight weeks old, but won't be nearly such an appealing idea when he's 70 pounds and covered in mud! Have a family meeting and agree on the house rules for your dog. It's much easier to prevent problems than to try to solve them later on.

Back to school

Regular attendance at an effective training school that has classes especially for puppies under the age of 18 weeks will get you off to a good start, and can be the perfect adjunct to all your efforts at home. A good puppy class will offer a combination of controlled play, and fun, gentle training. As your dog's owner, you are the most important factor in its life and this relationship will be built on and developed through the classes. Many puppy classes encourage the whole family to attend and can help you to learn about your dog's needs in an active and enjoyable way. Such classes are just like nursery schools for dogs and can lead to involvement in other canine sports, such as agility or advanced training.

What a puppy class can offer

● Puppies of a similar age — under 18 weeks — for your puppy to play and practice social skills with.

● An experienced instructor, who can help with training and behavioral difficulties.

● Like-minded owners, who will contribute to the socialization of all the puppies in the group, just by their presence, and through handling and petting.

● A friendly and safe environment in which both dogs and their owners can relax and enjoy controlled play with the puppy off the leash.

Housebreaking

Dogs are naturally clean creatures, and nearly all learn to be clean indoors very rapidly. But they need our help. Learn to predict when your puppy will need to relieve himself — after playing, after waking up, after any kind of excitement, and straight after meals. At these times, take your puppy to the same place outside and wait with him — even in the rain. Gently repeating a phrase, such as "Be quick," helps your puppy to remember why he's there. As soon as your puppy starts to sniff around, or circle, praise him very gently. Once he has relieved himself, lavish him with praise and give him a really special tidbit to reward him.

Going outdoors

Even if you're not sure he needs to, it is wise to take your puppy outside about once an hour. You should also watch him closely for signs that he might need to go, such as sniffing or circling. If you wait outside with your puppy and he does not relieve himself, bring him back inside. It is then up to you to supervise him. If you cannot watch him, you either need to put him in a crate or playpen, or in an enclosed area where you do not mind if he has an accident. The advantage of confining your puppy, for short periods, is that he will probably try to wait until you take him out again because he will not want to soil his sleeping area.

If you catch your puppy in the act of going in the house, or about to go, say "Outside" in an urgent voice, then take him outside quickly to show him where you do want him to go — even if it's too late to save your carpet! If he gets just one drop in the right place you can then praise your puppy.

Be patient

Being cross with your puppy for making a mistake in the house is pointless. Dogs soon learn to associate any mess with your anger — not with the act of going — and simply show fear when you find it. It takes years for a child to be fully toilet trained, but no one would consider punishing a baby for having an accident in an inappropriate place. Old-fashioned punishments, such as rubbing the dog's nose in its own mess, are abhorrent and counterproductive and should never be used.

Paper training

Many people use sheets of newspaper to teach their puppy to relieve himself where they want it. This is harder work in the long term, however, than the "errorless" approach because you need to housebreak your puppy twice — once to paper, and then again, outdoors.

Bite inhibition & night routines

Biting during play is normal and helps puppies discover what is alive and what is not. Puppies play together by biting each other and this is accepted happily until the pressure becomes too hard. It is vital that all puppies learn how to moderate their bites before they lose their deciduous (temporary) teeth at 18 weeks. This is known as "learning bite inhibition." Dogs that have learned good bite inhibition are more likely to be safe around adults, children, and other dogs later in life.

1 Your puppy needs to understand that biting hurts. Yelp loudly each and every time your puppy mouths your hands or clothes.

2 Immediately turn away as if to nurse your wounds, and ignore your puppy. Your puppy will probably look a little bewildered.

3 Ignore your puppy for about 20 seconds, then continue interacting. Repeat the "Ouch!" and turn away each and every time you feel his teeth.

4 Biting will not stop immediately, but it should become less and less hard over three to four weeks. At this point, your puppy will realize that he cannot put any pressure on you at all, and then you can yelp even if he puts his mouth on you gently.

5 Do not play rough-and-tumble games with your puppy, or play any game where the puppy grabs your clothes, skin, or hair. This is giving your puppy permission to bite and will set back all your other efforts. Use a toy to play with your puppy and end the game immediately if you feel his teeth.

Nighttime routines

Dogs are social creatures, and being separated from their family overnight can be traumatic, especially at first when a puppy is still used to the company of its mom and littermates. Decide where you want your dog to sleep, and don't give in. Make sure that your puppy has a cozy bed of his own and ensure that he learns to associate it with comfort and security. For this reason it is wise never to send your dog to his bed as a punishment. Instead, encourage him to settle into it several times during the day, and give him a chew toy to help establish positive associations. This routine can be especially useful during family mealtimes when you want your dog to settle down quietly.

Puppy crates

Puppy crates or cages can be a real sanity-saver, especially for nighttime use and to help with housebreaking. It may look like a jail, but introduced properly and made comfortable inside, a crate can be a cozy nest, away from the bustle of family life and a home-away-from-home when traveling. Many dogs love them so much that they will choose to sleep inside them. Some even learn to open and close the cage door.

Socialization

Each and every dog that lives with a family needs to be "domesticated" individually. Our pet dogs are descended from wolves, and although they differ in many ways from their wild cousins, they have not lost all their similarities. Research has shown that puppies who do not have contact with human beings before the end of the critical period (12 weeks of age), grow up to behave like wild dogs. These dogs never learn to trust humans, to enjoy their company, or to follow the basic obedience exercises that make dogs so much easier to live with.

What is socialization?

Socialization means learning a language and being able to communicate in that language with others, rather than ignoring them or becoming aggressive or defensive. A well-socialized puppy can "read" the body language and facial expressions of people and other dogs easily and quickly, and knows how to respond appropriately.

The 12-week wonder

Puppies learn how to communicate with other beings during a very short period of their development. This period, which lasts between 5 and 12 weeks of age, is so important that it is named "the critical period." Of course, puppies continue to learn after this time, but their whole outlook is likely to be affected by their experience and patterns of learning during this period. It's really the equivalent of the first five years of a child's life.

What you can do

The most vital help you can give your puppy to ensure that he is well-socialized during the critical period is to take him out to meet the world. Puppies desperately need to meet and mix with as many different people and dogs as possible to become fluent in communicating with body language.

From a puppy's perspective, all people look, smell, and sound different, and this means that while a puppy could become completely familiar with you and the other members of your family, he may become a quivering wreck when meeting someone new if he hasn't had the chance to generalize his experiences with other people.

Experience checklist

All puppies need to be exposed to these kinds of visual experiences in order to discover that human beings are safe to be with, no matter how they look. To help your puppy become familiar with other people and other dogs, he needs to meet and mix with as many of the people and dogs on the checklist below as possible:

- People of different ages
- People of different nationalities
- Children of different ages
- People wearing different clothing, such as hats, glasses, and gloves
- Men with beards
- Dogs of different ages, breeds, sizes, and colors

To a puppy, a human being wearing a crash helmet may look like a being from outer space, while children who have been to a carnival and have had their faces painted can be totally unrecognizable!

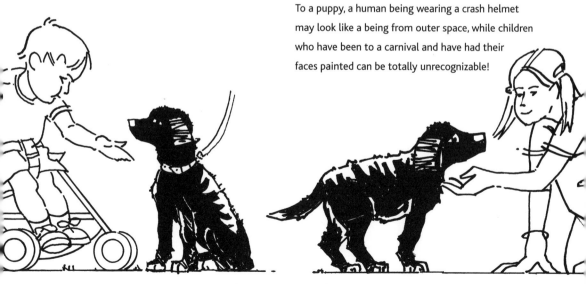

Action plan

In addition to learning how to relate to people and other dogs, it's essential that a puppy becomes familiar with everyday sights, sounds, and smells. In order to be confident with the world around them, puppies need to experience as many aspects of their environment as possible on a daily basis. The critical period for learning about the world ends at around 12 weeks of age, so time is short.

5–8 weeks of age

The chances are that your puppy still will be with the breeder during this time. This is the perfect opportunity for him to experience all kinds of domestic sights and sounds: the washing machine, the vacuum cleaner, even walking on different surfaces. Puppies also need to be handled by lots of different people during this time.

8–12 weeks of age

As soon as your puppy is home with you he needs to mix with as many people as possible and see the world around him. Even if he has not completed his vaccinations, he can be carried out and about to see and hear traffic, strollers, and the general hustle and bustle of life. Bear in mind that puppies need to be exposed to many different kinds of environments, particularly those that you may visit in the future. If you live in the countryside, practice trips to the town are vital, and vice versa.

Puppy experience checklist

In the home

- Vacuum cleaner
- Washing machine
- Hair dryer
- Telephone ringing
- Aerosol sprays
- Carpet
- Wooden floors
- Stairs
- Other pets

Outdoors

- Vehicles
- Bicycles
- Strollers
- The vet's office
- Walking on grass
- Walking on gravel
- Open spaces
- Town centers
- Buildings
- Crowds
- Joggers
- Livestock
- Airplanes

Traveling

Many puppies get carsick to begin with, but just like children, they grow out of it with time and practice. Short and frequent journeys in the car are essential for all puppies to get them accustomed to the motion of the vehicle. Take your puppy on the train or bus, too. The more that he experiences now, the more confident he will be with different forms of travel later.

Starting Off: An Adult Dog

Bringing a new adult dog into the home can be as exciting as getting a puppy, and the first days and weeks are just as formative. Be consistent right from the start, and with just 10 minutes of training a day you can look forward to many happy years ahead with your new companion.

The first two weeks for a dog in any new home are often described as the honeymoon period. This is because the dog will usually be on his best behavior, watching closely to learn about the family routines, and simply appreciating the security. After this time, many dogs start to test the water to see how firmly set the boundaries are. Some dogs will pester for attention, while others may challenge over toys or food.

Overdependency

Many dogs bond so closely to their owner during the honeymoon period that they could be described as overdependent. In the beginning, this can feel flattering. It is quite pleasant to think that your dog wants to be with you continually, even when you go to the bathroom. However, discovering that you can't go out and leave the dog, even for a few minutes, may well change your mind! Dogs that are overdependent on their owners may howl, bark, become destructive, or even mess in the house when left home alone. This is simply because they can't cope without their owner. Separation problems may be due to distress, frustration, or boredom. Some dogs may even be given to an animal shelter because of such a problem, but it is preventable.

Preventing overdependency

The following simple steps are designed to ensure that your dog is given love, attention, and security but does not become overdependent on you.

1 Try not to allow your dog to become "addicted" to you in the first couple of weeks. Give affection and attention when you decide to, not when he demands it.

2 Don't allow your dog to follow you from room to room. Shut doors between you and him as a part of your daily routine. Try not to allow constant contact when you are in the same room. Many dogs that later develop separation anxiety have a history of constantly needing to touch their owners in some way.

3 Practice trial separations. Encourage your dog to go to his resting place, give him something good to chew or play with, then leave. Leave your dog frequently for short periods throughout the day. This is particularly important if it is the school vacation or you have taken time off work to help the dog settle in, or it will be too much of a shock for your dog when the routine returns to normal.

4 Leave your dog with toys that are fun and rewarding to play with. Most dog toys are only amusing if a human is playing, too. However, it is quite possible to keep your dog entertained by himself with "interactive" toys — ones that reward the dog for playing with them. Hollow sterilized bones (that don't splinter), or a Kong® toy, can be filled with food so that the dog has to work to get it out. Safe chews, and other toys such as Activity Balls or Buster® Cubes (activity toys that dispense treats), also work well. To maintain the novelty value of these toys, save them for the times when you go out. Do not allow your dog to have them when you are home.

House rules

Some dogs have had a difficult time before finding themselves in a new home and with a new family. It can be tempting to overcompensate for their previous experiences, but starting afresh is the most positive way to overcome your new dog's past. Follow these suggestions to ensure that your dog is happy and secure.

Slave to affection?

Give your dog attention and affection when you decide. Most dogs are absolute masters at demanding attention from us whenever they like — usually in the middle of our favorite TV program! Fold your arms, look away, and ignore your dog if he is attention-seeking. However, give him plenty of quality time on your terms. Playing with him, grooming him, and giving him affection when you decide to will all help to strengthen the bond between you and your dog — and let him know that you are not his slave!

Back to basics

Don't assume that your new dog is housebroken just because he is an adult. Many rehomed dogs have never lived indoors before and may take time to get used to the new routine. Treat your dog as if he is a puppy and train him using rewards for relieving himself in the correct place. Never punish your dog if you have allowed him to make a mistake — it is counterproductive. There may be times when you simply cannot ignore a dog's inappropriate behavior. On these occasions, interrupt the behavior without giving the dog any attention. For example, ring the doorbell or rattle the cookie can. Then give your dog an alternative behavior that you can praise him for.

Fit for life

All dogs need exercise to stay fit and healthy, and to give them mental stimulation. Understimulated dogs can discover that chewing or destroying items in the house relieves their boredom. They may even add opening the refrigerator door to their list of challenges!

Two outings a day are usually considered ideal, but different dogs in different circumstances may need more or less. Walks should be as varied as possible to increase your dog's view of the world.

Food for thought

Arriving in a new home can be unsettling for some dogs, so don't be too concerned if he doesn't eat as well as you'd expect. It's best to stick to the food that your dog has been used to eating for awhile to avoid tummy upsets, and make sure that fresh water is always available. Don't tempt your new dog to eat by offering delicious extras or food from your plate. Dogs are very good at training people to pop to the supermarket to buy something different for dinner!

Training timetable

All dogs need and enjoy training, no matter what their age, breed, or ability. The training should be gentle, kind, and reward-based for your dog to really want to learn new tasks and exercises. Once your dog's motivation has been set, you can teach him almost anything. Just by spending 10 minutes each day on training, your dog will be able to master the basics quickly.

Step by step

Training progress is made in small steps, so start with simple behaviors for which your dog will enjoy being rewarded, and gradually build on your successes. If your dog has trouble with a certain exercise, go back to basics and reinforce what he already knows. Becoming impatient or angry will hinder your dog's training. Remember your first few driving lessons and the effect that stress can have on learning ability!

Super brains

Most dogs learn to respond quickly to the sound of at least 30 different words, but some super canine brains have been known to respond to 90!

Different breeds, different needs

Different breeds and types of dog will almost always find some exercises easier than others. For example, most herding dogs, such as collies, find walking to heel relatively simple, because in their minds they are herding you up while they walk next to you! On the other hand, retrievers will usually find fetching an easy task, because it's an instinctive behavior to pick up items and carry them around. You will need to be more patient when teaching an exercise that doesn't come naturally to your dog. Take your time and make sure that the whole training experience is an enjoyable one. Getting impatient can dampen your dog's enthusiasm for learning altogether.

The first week

● House training — your dog should be learning that relieving himself outdoors is rewarding!

● Clicker training — your dog should understand the concept of the clicker as a signal of reward.

● Attention — your dog should look at you when you say his name.

● Sit — your dog should understand the word "Sit" and obey the command at least 90 percent of the time.

● Down — your dog should be able to follow a lure and move into the down position with encouragement.

● Recall — your dog should come toward you in the home or yard when you call his name and encourage him.

● Whistle training — your dog should be starting to respond to the whistle that calls him for dinner. (For more about whistle training, *see pages 34–35*.)

The first month

● Sit — your dog should be able to respond to the word by sitting in all situations, no matter what the distraction.

● Down — your dog should be able to lie down on command without the need for a lure.

● Recall — your dog should be responding to the whistle when out and about on a long line or extending leash.

● Leave it — this command should be reliable for at least 10 seconds.

Basic Obedience Training

Dogs are capable of learning the most complex tasks and intricate tricks. Spending 10 minutes a day to get the basic exercises right will provide a strong foundation for training that will last a lifetime.

Teaching your dog to respond to the sound of his name may seem simple, but once your dog is outdoors, or is distracted, it can be the greatest training challenge of all! Puppies in particular can have a short span of concentration, so make sessions short and enjoyable — but frequent. Proceed gradually and teach your dog that his name means "Look at me!"

Attention training

Make sure that you and your dog are somewhere calm and quiet, such as your kitchen or the backyard. Have some tasty, small treats, such as cheese, sausage, or chicken at the ready. Hold the clicker behind your back to begin with. There is no need to point it at your dog, and you should avoid clicking too near his ears.

Changing names

Nearly all dogs from previous homes will have a name when they come to you. If you don't like this name, it's easy to change it. Follow the attention exercise and use your dog's new name at times when he will make pleasant associations with it. Most dogs learn their new name within a few days and forget their old one.

1 Say your dog's name in a happy voice. The chances are, your dog will look at you. If he doesn't, show him that you have a food reward to gain his interest.

2 As soon as he looks at you, click and give a reward.

3 Repeat this several times. It's important that you are generous at the outset of training. This will give your dog confidence and help him believe that training is fun.

Soon, your dog will start to understand the meaning of the clicker and will react to the sound, thinking, "Great, where's my treat?!"

Try the attention exercise

- In every room in your house.
- In the yard or garden.
- In your car.
- When your dog is snoozing — see if he wakes up and pays attention to you.
- On a leash in a busy place.

As your dog gets better at responding to you when you say his name, gradually fade out the number of rewards he gets for the behavior. Try to do this randomly, so your dog never knows if he is going to get a click and treat for giving you attention when you ask, or not. Vary the rewards he gets, too — sometimes a food treat, other times a game with a toy, or praise and affection.

"Sit" is probably the easiest command to teach your dog, and one of the most useful. There are literally hundreds of things your dog can't be doing if he's sitting — jumping up, digging in the backyard, and chasing the cat are just a few!

Sitting on command

1 Show your dog that you have a food treat in your hand. Holding it between your fingers, place the food close to his nose. Now lift your hand up and back, so your dog has to look right up toward the ceiling to follow your fingers. Looking upward like this causes a physical chain reaction — his rear end has to go down.

2 Watch carefully. If your dog's front legs come off the ground, your hand is a little too high. As soon as his bottom hits the ground, click, then give your dog the treat. Repeat this a few times to give your dog a chance to practice the movement.

3 Say the word "Sit" just before you move the food lure. Try to say the word only once, in a calm, quiet voice. Practice a few more times. Click and treat each time at the beginning to motivate him to continue. Bear in mind that if you repeat the command, your dog will anticipate that this is the cue that you are using. "Sit" is quite different from "Sit, sit, sit" to your dog.

5 Practice, practice, practice! Your dog will become really proficient at sitting when you ask if you repeat the training many times in a variety of different locations. Ask your dog to sit before he gets anything he likes — his dinner, having his leash put on, or being let out into the backyard. This also helps to encourage the behavior and is a polite way for your dog to say "Please" and "Thank you."

4 Now, you need to phase out the food lure. With no food in your hand, ask your dog to sit. If he does so, click immediately, then give a food treat. If your dog does not sit when asked, help him with the hand signal, then reward for good efforts. Allow your dog thinking time. If he seems hesitant, be patient and just wait for the correct response. He needs to use his brain to get the rewards.

Down

The "Down" command requires a little more patience than "Sit." Most dogs love lying down on command once they get the hang of it. Be patient and your dog will soon be responding to one quiet command.

Teaching your dog to lie down on command

1 Ask your dog to sit. Now, hold the food treat close to your dog's nose, then lower your hand very slowly right down to the floor, directly between the dog's front paws. Hang onto the treat by turning your palm down, with the food hidden inside your hand. This way, the dog will want to burrow his nose underneath, and he will turn his head sideways to nibble at it.

2 Be patient and keep your hand still if you can. Some dogs try other behaviors before they finally lie down, so persistence pays.

3 The instant your dog lies down, click, then — most importantly — drop the treat onto the floor and let the dog eat it. (This prevents the dog from following your hand back up again like a yo-yo!)

4 Repeat this several times, sometimes with the food in your hand, sometimes without. Once you can guarantee that your dog will lie down by following your hand to the floor, you can say "Down," just before you lure him into position.

5 Now stand up straight. Quietly, ask your dog to "Down," but this time don't help him with a hand signal. Most dogs will try several other behaviors before having the idea that lying down might work. Be patient and keep quiet. If his attention wanders, keep showing your dog that food and toy rewards are on offer. The instant that your dog lies down, click, then give a jackpot reward — several tasty treats and a game!

6 Repeat this around the house and yard, on the leash and off, until your dog is responding reliably anywhere and everywhere to the word "Down." Once this is happening, you no longer need to use the clicker and rewards each time. Instead, use praise and smiles and just the occasional treat — your dog still needs to know that he's done the right thing.

Come when called

I t's vital that your dog learns to come to you when you call or whistle. Indoors, it's generally easier to call your dog by name, but whistle training can have many advantages when outdoors, as the sound carries further than your voice and the signal is always consistent.

Responding to a whistle

Contrary to popular belief, dogs do not respond automatically to any kind of whistle. Instead, they need to learn to associate the sound with good things, such as food and toys. The easiest way to do this is to pair the sound of the whistle with your dog's mealtimes.

1 Prepare your dog's food, so that he knows good things are coming!

2 Hold the bowl above his head so that he sits in front of you.

3 Blow the whistle. Most people use two or three short, sharp blasts.

4 Give your dog his dinner immediately. Repeat the routine at every mealtime for at least a week to enable your dog to understand properly the connection between the two events.

Now move onto whistling the dog to you in the house.

1 Have another family member hold your dog a short distance from you.

2 Show him that you have some delicious food treats or a toy.

3 Give the same signal on the whistle that you do at feeding time, then allow the dog to be released and come to you for his reward.

Once your dog is proficient at this exercise in the house, take your dog outside into a safe, fenced area, such as the backyard. Go through the same routine, but make sure that your rewards are good ones.

When your dog is reliable in the yard, you can begin to practice the same exercise out on walks. Try to set up the first few recalls to ensure that they are successful. Use a long line or extending leash if you feel unsure and always give lots of praise and treats when your dog responds to the whistle.

Recall problems

Once your dog has learned to come when whistled, click and treat him for coming to you on occasion, to keep the response strong and quick.

● Don't call your dog if you think he will ignore you, for example, when he's about to play with another dog.
● Make your walks out together fun. If you are talking on your cell and ignoring your dog, you can't be surprised that he's ignoring you. Play with your dog, vary the routes you take, and make sudden changes of direction to keep him interested.

Recall training tip
Be consistent with your use of the whistle. This is particularly important in the early stages of training where the dog needs to learn the association between the sound of the whistle and his rewards.

Leave

This is an extremely useful command. Puppies are like toddlers, and like to explore the world by picking things up with their mouths to check how they taste and feel. Teaching your dog not to touch items can be a real life-saver, and will save your sanity, too!

Leaving on command

Before you teach your dog the "Leave" command, make sure you are somewhere calm and quiet. Keep your dog on the leash if he is likely to wander off or become distracted. This exercise requires your dog's brain to be engaged!

1 Hold a treat in your hand and close your fingers around it tightly. Present your hand to your dog and wait while he sniffs, licks, and nibbles, trying to get the food. Do not say anything.

2 Watch carefully. As soon as your dog takes his nose away from your hand, even for a split second, click, then release the treat. Repeat this several times. Most dogs learn to take their mouths away from your hand in about four tries.

3 Now repeat the exercise, but this time wait until he has taken his nose away from your hand to the count of three, then click and treat. Build up the amount of time that your dog will wait with his nose well away from your hand to about 10 seconds. At this point you can add in the command, "Leave," in a calm, quiet voice.

4 Once your dog has got the hang of this, repeat the exercise, but this time say "Leave," then present the food on your open hand. If your dog tries to take it, simply close your fingers around the food — do not jerk your hand away.

Stay

The "Stay" command is all about trust. Your dog needs to have confidence that you will not leave him, so build up the exercise gradually and build on your success with fun variations on the command.

Staying on command

Once your dog has learned to sit or lie down on command reliably, you can teach him to stay in that position for longer, by varying the length of time before you click and treat, and by adding in distractions.

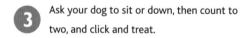
1 Ask your dog to sit or down, count to five, then click and treat.

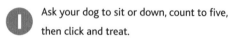
2 Ask your dog to sit or down, then count to 10 and click, then treat.

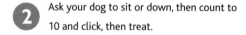
3 Ask your dog to sit or down, then count to two, and click and treat.

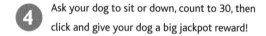
4 Ask your dog to sit or down, count to 30, then click and give your dog a big jackpot reward!

Building on the exercise

Make sure that you keep your dog in position for random amounts of time — and build up to about two minutes. Praise all the time he is sitting or lying down. The click ends the behavior, so make sure that you click while the dog is still sitting or lying down, then treat two to three seconds later.

Now add in some distractions. These should be fairly gentle to start with. If your dog moves, then you know that you have done too much too soon. Go back to a simpler task and build up the distractions once again until you achieve success.

Try these for fun

● With your dog sitting, take two paces away from him. Then move back to him, praise, and click and treat.

● Ask your dog to lie down. Put your hands on your head. If he stays, click and treat him.

● Keep your dog sitting in one place while you take off one shoe and then put it back on again.

● Ask your dog to lie down, then sit in your favorite armchair while you count to 50. Return to your dog before clicking and giving him a treat.

● Ask your dog to sit, and walk all around him while he stays sitting.

● Here's a real test. With your dog lying down, see if you can lie down on the floor next to him, then get up again. Give big rewards for staying.

Walking on & off a leash

Dogs soon figure out that by pulling, they get to the park more quickly, and can lead their owner wherever they want to go, rather than the other way around. Dogs need to be told that they are in the right place when walking nicely on the leash. This is where the clicker comes into its own. Rather than scolding the dog for pulling, take away his fun by standing still. When the dog is in the right place, let him know by clicking and treating, and moving forward. The main reason why so many dogs pull on the leash is that they get rewarded for it.

Walking on a leash without pulling

1 Put your dog on the leash in the living room, hallway, or backyard. Stand still to begin with.

2 As soon as your dog puts slack in the leash and looks at you, click and treat, then start walking in any direction you choose.

3 Watch your dog's position carefully. If there is tension in the leash, stand still or suddenly change direction. Do not take one single step in the direction your dog wants to go if the leash is tight.

4 Every time there is a loop in the leash, click and treat.

5 Repeat this a few times, then stop and have a game. Be generous with the food to begin with, then gradually reward only the best responses.

Once this is reliable, you can begin to practice outside on walks. Don't expect too much too soon. You may stand still more than you walk forward, but be patient. On days when you are in a hurry, use a head collar (a collar that fits on the dog's head with the leash attachment underneath — like a pony halter) or a body harness to prevent pulling from becoming a habit. Click and treat when your dog is in the right place while wearing the head collar to hasten your training.

Walking to heel — off-leash

It's excellent practice to encourage your dog to walk to heel off-leash with you. For safety, do this in an enclosed area away from roads, in case your dog becomes distracted.

1 Show your dog that you have a food treat, and encourage him to follow you to get it.

2 Click and treat when he's next to your leg. This can be on either the left or right side, but pick one side and be consistent.

3 Change direction frequently so that your dog has to play "tag" and catch you. Only when he does should you click and treat.

4 Add in your command when your dog is reliably walking next to you in the correct position. "Heel" or "Close" are commonly used.

5 Gradually fade out the number of clicks and treats that your dog receives, but praise him when he does well.

Correctional devices

All dogs can be taught to walk nicely on an ordinary flat collar and leash or head collar and leash. Choke chains, prong collars, or other so-called "correctional" devices are totally unnecessary and can easily cause injury. There's no substitute for good training and practice.

Overcoming Bad Habits

Behavior problems in dogs can seriously affect the quality of life for both dogs and owners. Nearly all bad habits can be prevented or modified, so act quickly to ensure that they don't become established.

Fear

Problem: My dog is frightened of loud noises, like thunder and fireworks. He cowers down, pants heavily, and salivates. I've tried to reassure him but it doesn't seem to help.

Solution: Dogs can suffer a great deal of fear and stress by hearing fireworks or other loud noises. Some may bark or whine, others may run away, hide under furniture, or try to get reassurance from their owners. In really severe cases, dogs may tremble and salivate.

It may be instinctive to comfort your pet when he is anxious. However, this is problematic because your dog will regard cuddles and soothing words as a reward for being fearful.

To overcome your dog's fear of loud noises:
● Ignore any signs of fear. Don't look at, touch, or talk to your dog — no matter how tempting!
● Put the TV or radio on and behave as you would normally.
● Give your dog something positive to do. For example, play a game, do some training with tasty treats, or give him a toy or chew.

Nervousness

Problem: My puppy is frightened and nervous of other people. Whenever I have friends and visitors over, he tries to hide behind me and will run away if he gets the chance.

Solution: Nervousness is a coping strategy that is usually due to lack of experience. In a situation that frightens him, a dog that has not learned how to cope in any other way may crouch down, ears flattened to his head, tail tucked underneath his body, and may try to slink away. Some dogs may even try to hide behind their owners.

If such anxiety is not addressed, nervousness may lead the dog to use aggression as a defensive strategy. Ideally, all puppies should be outgoing and confident in new situations. This means that they will be less inclined to run away or use aggression.

Substantial socialization is urgently required for any puppy showing this behavior. Get your puppy out and about to meet as many people as possible, but without overwhelming him. Your puppy needs to form positive associations with new people, so giving them treats to drop on the ground close to your puppy can work well.

Gradually build up to allow other people to touch and stroke your puppy — but don't rush him too much. Ignore fearful behavior if possible — don't look at him, talk to him, or touch him — and praise and reward confident behaviors instead.

Chewing & destructive behavior

Chewing

Problem: Our dog chews the furniture and anything else he can get hold of. He has his own toys so we can't understand why he's chewing our things.

Solution: All dogs need to chew. Puppies particularly need to ease the discomfort of inflamed gums around teething time, and may also have a secondary "teething" period at around six to eight months when the adult teeth establish themselves firmly into the jaw bone. Chewing may also release "feel-good" chemicals into the brain, meaning that some dogs may chew to reassure themselves when left alone.

Sadly, dogs do not know the difference between a stick and a table leg, nor an old slipper and a brand new sneaker. They're all chew toys to them!

Give your dog plenty of safe chew toys, such as the tug toy provided in this pack. Toys that reward the dog for chewing them are ideal. Hollow rubber chew toys stuffed with food are specially designed so that small pieces of food come out while the dog is chewing, making the experience even more rewarding. If your dog is chewing and ingesting inappropriate items, check to ensure that his diet is suiting him. Some dogs also chew to relieve boredom, or frustration, so make sure you are giving your dog enough exercise and mental stimulation overall.

Destructive behavior

Problem: My dog suffers horribly when I go out and leave him. He gets very upset and has destroyed my carpet and baseboards by chewing and scratching at them.

Solution: Dogs that can't be left home alone are nearly always overdependent on their owners. If your dog follows you around the house when you are home and acts like your shadow, you may be storing up future overdependency problems that could result in destructive behavior, barking, or indoor toileting.

Right from the start of your relationship with your dog, make sure that you leave him on his own frequently for short periods of time — even if you are in the house with him. Leave him in a safe place, such as the kitchen or an indoor crate with some wonderfully rewarding toys to chew and play with that he never has at any other time. Leave your dog for only a few minutes to begin with, then build up to a couple of hours. Most dogs accept this quite happily once they become secure in the knowledge that you are going to return. Seek professional help if your dog can't bear to be parted from you for even a minute. The earlier you sort this problem out, the better.

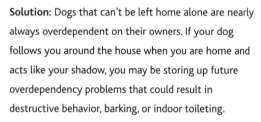

Jumping up & pulling on leash

Jumping up

Problem: Our dog is very friendly, but he jumps up at visitors, making a mess of their clothes. He's a big dog, and we're worried he might knock someone down.

Solution: As jumping up is usually friendly behavior, particularly in puppies, it is totally inappropriate to use any kind of aversive technique to prevent it. Instead, think about what you would prefer your dog to do when greeting people — either keeping all four feet on the ground, or even better, sitting. Teaching "sit to greet" is relatively simple.

First, make sure that all jumping up of any kind at home is ignored. Turn your back and fold your arms if your dog jumps up. Praise and pet him if he is sitting or being calm. Then, ask a friend to help. Put your dog on a leash. When your friend arrives, ask them to ignore your puppy completely to begin with. Both of you must ignore all attempts to gain attention by jumping up. When your dog tires of bouncing, and offers a sit or down, click, praise, and give a food treat. Your friend can then praise and pet your dog, but must instantly stand up and turn away again if he jumps up. This kind of training requires total consistency. Banish anyone from your home who says the terrible words, "I don't mind!"

Pulling on the leash

Problem: Our dog pulls so hard on the leash that we're worried he's going to choke himself! This makes taking him for a walk very difficult, so he's getting less exercise.

Solution: Dogs pull on the leash for many different reasons. The main one is usually that we inadvertently reward them for doing it by going where they want to — and at his pace. Unfortunately, this is so rewarding for dogs that it is not something they grow out of. Indeed, the more practice they have at the behavior, the better they get at it.

Follow the training section (*see pages 40–41*) to get your heelwork practice underway. If your dog is a truly persistent puller, using a correctly fitted head collar such as a Gentle Leader, or a body harness, can help. Consistency is important in this exercise so this is one way you can ensure that your dog never gets the chance to pull. These are aids however, and should always be used in conjunction with the training. Never use choke/check chain collars or prong collars — these are unnecessarily punitive, and can cause severe damage to your dog.

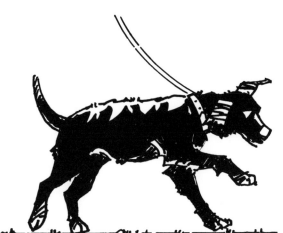

Stealing & guarding

Stealing

Problem: Our dog will steal almost anything he can get his paws on: shoes, the kids' toys, pens, and even the TV remote control. Once he has gotten hold of them, he'll dash to the bottom of the yard and refuse to give them up.

Solution: Stealing items from around the house and running off with them is dog sport. Unfortunately, it can lead to problems later on if it is encouraged at an early age. Think about this behavior from your dog's point of view. There he is, lying on the carpet, being ignored. He chews on a dog toy. Still, he is ignored. Bored, he wanders over to your glasses case. He picks it up. Suddenly, the whole household descends on him! He runs and a great game of chase ensues! Guess which of the items — dog toy or glasses case — he will choose again next time he wants something to do?

Put away items of value. Make sure that your puppy cannot get hold of your most precious things. Puppies especially love socks, hair scrunchies, pens, and shoes.

If your puppy picks up something he should not have, but you can sacrifice it, then do. Washcloths, tea towels, and tissues can all be ignored. Stand up and walk out of the room to show you really don't care.

If you cannot walk away, DO NOT CHASE your dog for the item, or shout. Instead, call him to you, praise him, and give him a tidbit in return for the item.

Work on teaching your dog to fetch items to you. This utilizes his natural instincts and will keep him out of trouble.

Guarding

Problem: Our dog is inclined to growl when we go near his food bowl. We are worried that he might become aggressive if the children go near him while he's eating.

Space for feeding

If you have more than one dog, make sure you give them lots of space when they are eating, or feed them in separate rooms if one dog eats more quickly than the other. Nothing causes tensions between dogs more quickly than disputes over food, and prevention is much better than cure.

Solution: Dogs need to know that humans are safe to be around when they are eating, and that we don't present a threat to their food. Unfortunately, many owners teach their dogs to be aggressive around their bowl by taking their food away. If someone tried to steal your dinner, you'd want to defend your meal. Dogs are not so different.

Adding food to your dog's dish while he is eating is a great way to reassure him that you are no threat. To do this, simply toss in extra pieces of food while your dog is eating, then walk away. If you repeat this behavior often enough, most dogs soon come to welcome your presence at mealtimes as they might get something extra.

Advanced Obedience Training

Y ou've established the basics, and now your dog is ready for more. Playing with your dog is essential. It builds bonds between you, establishes social boundaries, and can be a wonderful motivator for training.

Different dogs like to play in different ways. For example, collies and other herding types usually love playing chase games, which is an extension of their ability to round up sheep and other animals. Not surprisingly, gundogs (dogs trained to work with hunters) like picking things up and carrying them around, while terriers often enjoy "killing" games where they can catch and shake a toy in their mouths.

Think about the type of toy that your dog would like to play with. Balls are fun for chasing, but don't offer any opportunity for tugging. Tug toys, such as the one included in this pack, are fun but only if a human is on the other end. Squeaky toys can drive some dogs crazy with excitement, but be careful that he doesn't eat the squeaker! Find out what your dog likes by offering him different types of toys. These don't have to be expensive. An empty plastic water bottle with dog biscuits inside can provide hours of entertainment.

Play safe

Playing with your dog needs to be fun and exciting for both of you — and it also needs to be safe. Dogs can move much faster than humans, and it is easy for accidents to happen if you don't play by the rules.

Always use a toy when playing with your dog. Never allow your dog to wrestle with you or bite your hands, clothes, or hair because this is giving your dog implicit permission to bite humans. Toys need to be long enough to keep your fingers out of the way (stop the game immediately if you feel your dog's teeth).

Tug games are fine, but keep the toy low to the ground when playing. This prevents the dog from jumping up to get the toy.

Teach your dog to drop the toy using one quiet command. This is easily done and all those who play with the dog should know how to get him to release the toy instantly, especially children.

Stop the game immediately if your dog touches your skin with his teeth or gets overexcited. Dogs need to learn that they can still have fun while controlling themselves around people.

Safety first

Many dogs each year are injured by playing with inappropriate items. Sticks may look like fun, but they can easily become lodged in the back of your dog's throat and can cause severe damage. Balls, too, can block your dog's airway if they are too small — and toys that are easily torn apart can present a risk if they are swallowed. Always supervise your dog with new toys until you are sure they are safe for him to play with.

Body language

Many dogs like to growl when they are playing with their owners. Watch your dog's body language closely. As long as his demeanor is telling you that he is only playing, this is nothing to worry about. However, if he goes still while playing or shows his teeth to you, stop immediately.

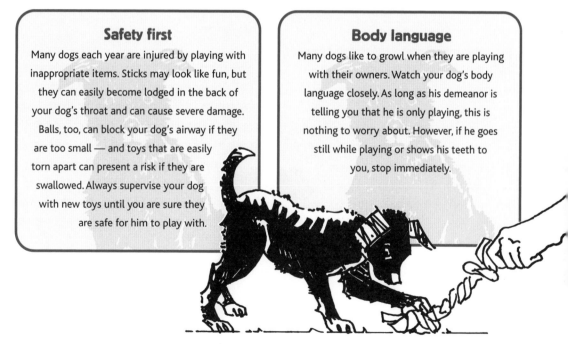

Fetch & drop

Teach your dog to be a reliable retriever and a whole world of training and exercise opportunities will suddenly become available to you and your pet. After all, why fetch the TV remote yourself when your dog can do it instead?

Retrieving on command

When you train your dog to retrieve, you are not teaching him to run out and pick something up, but to hold objects and give them to you.

1 Start with a toy or object that your puppy likes. This can be a rag, a cardboard tube, or a dog toy.

2 Have some tasty tidbits ready. Holding the object in your hand, offer it to the puppy to sniff. If he even touches it, click, or use your clicker word, then treat. Repeat this a few times. Now wait for something a little more. This time you are looking for the puppy to try to take the object in his mouth. If he does, let him hold it for one second, then click and treat.

3 Build up the time he will hold the object to about 20 seconds, then click and treat. Add the cue word "Hold," just before he takes it, when he starts to be reliable.

4 Next, you can put the object on your knee or on the floor and ask him to hold. Once you have mastered this, no matter where the object is, your dog will understand that "Hold" means go and pick it up, and bring it back for a click and treat. Usually, dogs find playing with toys like this so rewarding in itself that the clicks and treats can be phased out very quickly. Then the dog will play retrieve games just for the fun of it.

Dropping a toy on command

This is a great nonconfrontational way of teaching even the most passionate doggy player to drop a toy on command.

1 Have a really good game of tug with your dog. Make sure that he is genuinely involved in the game with you.

2 Hold onto the toy, but relax so that you are not putting any counterpressure against it. At the same time, drop a really yummy food treat on the floor in front of your dog.

3 Hold the toy still while your dog eats the food treat, then immediately play with him again. Most dogs are paranoid that you will snatch the toy away — so simply keep it there until he's ready to play again.

4 Repeat this several times. Say "Drop," in a quiet tone, just before he lets go of the toy and eats the food.

5 Practice this routine until your dog will let go of the toy reliably when you say "Drop," in anticipation of his treat.

6 Now practice this exercise by swapping one toy for another, as well as swapping the toy for food. Your dog should automatically let go of the toy on one quiet command from you to "Drop." At this stage, other people can practice the same behavior with your dog.

Hide & seek

No matter what breed of dog you own, his sense of smell is highly advanced — and is much better than our own. Dogs use scent to gain information about the world around them. In fact, they "read" scents left by other dogs just as we might read the paper. This explains why dogs like to sniff each other — and us!

Searching and tracking

The dog's incredible sense of smell makes him capable of locating items and people by following a scent trail — sometimes over incredible distances. All dogs are capable of this, but some breeds have been selectively bred to enhance their tracking instincts. Bloodhounds and beagles are good trackers.

Dogs use their sense of smell to stimulate themselves mentally. Teaching your dog to search or track for food, objects, or people can be very rewarding for both you and your pet, because it is one area where the dog clearly has a strong advantage over us, making us reliant on them and their heightened olfactory instincts and abilities.

Teaching your dog to hunt for food

These basic exercises will encourage your dog to hunt for food as a foundation to more complex tasks.

● Hide some tidbits under an old mug turned upside down. Encourage your dog to find the food by himself.

● Leave your dog in one room while you hide a toy or biscuit in another. Make the searches easy to begin with, keep the encouragement up, and give plenty of praise when he finds the item.

● You can then make the game harder by hiding a special item. Some dogs can be trained to search for a specific smell, such as a teabag.

● Hold your dog in one room while another family member hides. Send your dog to find them. This can also work well out on walks so your dog has to hunt for the person using his sense of smell.

Basic tracking

1 To teach your dog to track, you will first need to lay a simple trail for him to follow. This is best done first thing in the morning so that the scent track you leave is as fresh as possible. Go without your dog into the yard or field. Laying a trail on grass is much easier for your puppy than on a hard surface, because he will also be able to follow the scent of crushed vegetation.

2 Place a pole or marker on the ground, then walk in a straight line from the marker for only 10 paces. Put something tempting — food or a toy — on the ground as soon as you stop, then walk back over exactly the same footsteps that you have already taken.

3 Leave the track for about 10 minutes, then take your dog out on a leash to find the starting point.

4 Let him lead you toward the reward, and then play or allow him to eat the food when he finds it. At first, many dogs want to look for the reward rather than sniffing for it, so use your hand to encourage the dog to look at the ground and use his nose. Gradually make the trails longer as your dog gains confidence.

Backyard obstacle courses

Dogs love to run and jump, and just like children, they need physical exercise to keep fit and healthy, and out of trouble. Teaching your dog to negotiate a series of obstacles, or doing some agility training is a great way of improving control over your dog while enjoying the teamwork required between you.

Fun agility

It's simple to create a set of basic obstacles in your own backyard, or even in your home. Build your dog's confidence slowly and gently and never force your dog to do anything that he doesn't want to. Remember, he can't tell you if he's uncomfortable or frightened.

Milk carton slalom

1 Place six markers, such as milk cartons filled with sand, in a straight line, about 24 inches (60 cm) apart.

2 With your dog on or off the leash, see if you can get him to zigzag in and out of the markers without touching them. Start this by encouraging him to follow your hand with a food lure, then gradually fade it out.

3 Once your dog is an expert at this, you can move on to the advanced stage by placing toys or food treats on top of the markers. Your dog then has to resist touching these or knocking them off as he trots through.

See-saw

Teach your dog to walk along a plank of wood (about 10 inches/25 cm wide by 60 inches/150 cm in length) on the ground by encouraging him to follow a food treat in your hand.

Now, balance the plank on an old brick, so that it is only about 3 inches (8 cm) off the ground. Gently lure your dog onto the plank. Of course, it will then tip slightly so you need to give your dog lots of encouragement to give him confidence.

Once on the plank, the dog's weight will tip the other end slightly down again, so help him if you need to. Although the sensation of the movement surprises some dogs at the outset, once they understand that they can control it by using their own body weight, most dogs can't get enough!

Mini-hurdles

Balance bamboo poles on the top of upturned flowerpots to make a set of mini-hurdles in the backyard. Lure your dog over the hurdles with a food treat, or throw a toy to encourage him to hop over the jump. Click and treat as soon as he does.

Once your dog is confident with this, add more jumps and arrange them among the other obstacles to make a mini-course. See if you can both get a clear round!

Tunnel test

1 Start with one dining room chair, and encourage your dog to crawl underneath the legs. Use a food lure to begin with, but as soon as your dog understands the concept, give praise and a game instead.

2 Once your dog is proficient at scooting under the chair on command, line another chair up next to it and practice some more.

3 Gradually add to the number of chairs until they form a tunnel that your dog can run through. Clicker training helps here, because you can click as your dog runs through the tunnel, then reward him afterward.

Spin & give a paw

Teaching your dog tricks is a fun way to increase his overall training repertoire and build control. It also allows your dog to show off, which means your dog will receive eye contact, praise, and affection from other people, too.

Spin

The object of this trick is to get the dog to circle his body in a tight curve to the right or left, so that he'll circle on command as if he's chasing his tail. Apart from being a cute trick, it's a great way to get your dog to wipe his feet on a mat after he's been outdoors.

1 Hold a food treat in your fingers and encourage your dog to follow it around in a wide circle, so that his head nearly meets his tail. Click and treat at the end of the circle.

2 Repeat this until your dog is really comfortable and starts to predict the movement to get his reward.

3 At this point, lure your dog around with your hand, but without having a food treat in it. Click and treat for good responses.

4 Finally, use only a minimal hand signal to get your dog to circle around. Say the word "Spin" just before you help him. Be generous with your rewards and you'll find that very soon you won't need to show him what to do at all — he'll respond to the cue word alone.

Give a paw

1 Ask your dog to sit. Let him know that you have some food in your hand, but keep it tightly clenched in your fist, close to the floor.

2 Be ready to click, and give a treat, the instant your dog moves his paw. Most dogs will initially attempt to get the food by licking or nibbling at your hand. However, if you hang onto the food, most will then try a different tactic, by touching your hand with a paw. Click and treat immediately. Repeat this several times.

3 Now watch out for deliberate moves by your dog to offer his paw to you. Click and treat each time.

4 Finally, only click and reward for full attempts at shaking hands!

Breaking the ice

Tricks are a great way to introduce your dog to children because they are nonthreatening and help to break the ice in new social situations.

Roll over

Rock 'n' roll

This is a really neat trick that also allows you to groom the dog's belly without a struggle!

1 Ask your dog to lie down on command. Your dog needs to be lying comfortably, so that one leg is tucked underneath him. Using a food treat, lure your dog into turning his head as if to look over his own shoulder. Click and treat.

2 Now lure again, but this time hold onto the treat until his head has moved further and his shoulders twist so that he flops over onto his back.

3 Follow through with your hand until your dog has rolled all the way over. Praise, and click and treat.

4 Repeat this movement several times, then do the same without the food treat in your hand. Say "Roll over" just before you encourage him to roll.

5 Practice the trick until your dog can roll over from a standing start.

Lessons for life

Dogs are wonderful creatures. They can act as our eyes and ears, and as teammates and working partners. However, most of all, they are our companions and an integral part of our families. Spending just 10 minutes a day on teaching your dog to respond to basic commands will not only make day-to-day living enjoyable for you both, but will also serve to enhance a lifelong relationship between you.

Lifelong education

The more you can teach your dog, the more freedom you will be able to give him. There's no need to use force or compulsion when training your dog — understanding your dog's natural behavior and instincts will lead to far better results. Using kind, fair, and effective methods will allow you to build on your dog's basic training exercises and design a teaching program that suits your lifestyle, time, and your dog's temperament and behavior: truly lessons for life.

Web Sites & Further Reading

www.dogtrain.co.uk

Fact sheets, books, and products that give guidance on training your dog using kind, fair, and effective methods.

www.clickandtreat.com

Clicker training ideas and products.

www.clickertraining.com

Information and help in training your dog.

www.clickersolutions.com

More inspiration for the clicker trainer.

www.apdt.com

The Association of Pet Dog Trainers.

The Culture Clash
Jean Donaldson (James & Kenneth, 1997)

Diary of a Dotty Dog Doctor
John Fisher (Bantam, 1997)

Don't Shoot the Dog
Karen Pryor (Bantam, revised edition, 1999)

Puppy Training for Kids
Sarah Whitehead (Barron's Educational, 2001)

Index

Index

Acknowledgments

Many thanks to my colleagues at the Centre of Applied Pet Ethology (COAPE) for their ongoing support in the field of research and education.

Thanks also to my own dogs, Windsor and Tao, for their inspiration and their patience in waiting for walks!